W9-DDK-117

• KYLE WICKWARE'S •
MAKE YOUR OWN WORKING PAPER
LOCOMOTIVE

A CUT-AND-ASSEMBLE MODEL
OF A MINIATURE STEAM LOCOMOTIVE

PERENNIAL LIBRARY

HARPER & ROW, PUBLISHERS, New York

Cambridge, Philadelphia, San Francisco, Washington
London, Mexico City, São Paulo, Singapore, Sydney

MAKE YOUR OWN WORKING PAPER LOCOMOTIVE. Copyright ©
1986 by Kyle Wickware. All rights reserved. Printed in the
United States of America. No part of this book may be used or
reproduced in any manner whatsoever without written permission except in the case of brief quotations embodied in critical
articles and reviews. For information address Harper & Row,
Publishers, Inc., 10 East 53rd Street, New York, N.Y. 10022.
Published simultaneously in Canada by Fitzhenry & Whiteside
Limited, Toronto.

FIRST EDITION

Design by Jennie Nichols/Function thru Form

Illustrations by Guilbert Gates/Function thru Form

ISBN: 0-06-096105-8

86 87 88 89 90 10 9 8 7 6 5 4 3 2 1

INTRODUCTION

The invention of the practical steam engine in 1765 by James Watt brought with it revolutionary concepts that changed the history of the world. One such concept was the harnessing of steam power in a locomotive.

The steam locomotive is one of mankind's greatest mechanical creations and achievements—a symbol of speed, power and ingenuity. For the people of the Victorian era, the earliest locomotives were a thrilling and awesome sight. The steam locomotive changed the world in just a few short years. It could perform unbelievable tasks. It could pull a tremendous amount of weight, whether transporting cargo such as iron ore or hauling passengers. As more and more improvements were made, the cost of producing and operating the locomotive became more efficient and the speed of travel increased.

As railways expanded and the number of steam locomotives grew, so did civilization. The United States of America is probably the best example of a country built up by such expansion.

In this book you are invited to recreate, with your own hands, one of the first styles of steam locomotives ever built.

ABOUT
THE STEAMLESS
STEAMER

The model you are about to create is called a "steamless" steamer: It uses air pressure stored in a balloon in place of steam, but is in all other regards a real steam locomotive.

This model is powered by dual cylinders. Air pressure is allowed into the cylinder of your locomotive through a valve. This pressure forces the piston inside the cylinder to move. The piston is connected by a piston rod to the crankshaft, which is forced by the movement of the piston and rod to rotate. When the piston has traveled the length of the cylinder and can be pushed no further by the air pressure, the momentum of the wheel attached to the crankshaft causes the crankshaft to keep rotating. The piston is forced to travel back to the beginning point and the air trapped in the cylinder is allowed to escape. This completes the cycle. At this point, the intake valve opens again and thus another cycle begins. These cylinders are synchronized so that when one cylinder is receiving air, the other is exhausting air, providing continuous power.

The design of the cylinders and valves of your locomotive is one of the oldest types. It is called a "wobble cylinder" because the cylinder wobbles, or moves, when the engine runs. The motion of the cylinder is used to operate the valve which allows air pressure to enter the cylinder and trapped air to escape. It is a simple idea that works well.

Your model is not a simulation but a real working locomotive that you should find both educational and entertaining.

CONSTRUCTION OF THE STEAMLESS STEAMER

CAUTION: THE CONSTRUCTION OF THIS KIT REQUIRES THE USE OF SHARP CUTTING TOOLS AND "SUPER GLUE." THESE TOOLS AND THIS TYPE OF GLUE CAN BE DANGEROUS IF NOT HANDLED CAREFULLY. ADULT SUPERVISION IS SUGGESTED.

MATERIALS AND TOOLS

Before starting construction, assemble the following items:

A rubber band: It should be thin and small, not the large, flat type.

6 paper clips: Just about any type will work well. You may also use piano wire of the same size; about eighteen inches is needed.

3 toothpicks: The round, wood type, not a flat one. You may substitute the stem of a Q-Tip if it is made of wood.

A ballpoint-pen refill: The standard straight type, not a tapered one. This will serve as a form for the valve holes and for making air tubes.

A needle: The large sewing type. This is used for transferring marks to the reverse side of parts. You may also use the metal point of a drawing compass.

A hobby knife: The X-Acto with a 5/16″ shaft diameter is the proper size. A #11 blade is handy for cutting and scoring. You will use the handle for forming the cylinders. You may substitute a section of 5/16″ dowel that is smooth and straight.

A metal-edged ruler: This item is optional but is very handy as a guide for your knife when cutting out or scoring parts. The metal edge prevents the hobby knife from cutting into the ruler. A corkbacked ruler is ideal to prevent slipping.

Sandpaper: 150 grit; a coarser grit will not leave a smooth surface.

3 straight pins.

Graphite: Powdered or flaked graphite is used for lubrication.

2 Balloons: 9″ size. Better quality (heavier) balloons work much better. Try different brands to find which give the best results.

Paper glue: Almost any white paper glue will work well. Do not use clear fast-drying plastic model cement.

"Super glue."

Scissors: You need a good sharp pair. Cheap ones tend to tear rather than cut.

Pliers: Needle-nose with side cutters are best. You will use them to cut and bend the paper clips.

Cutting board: A thick section of cardboard is ideal. It needs to be hard and flat to provide a good working surface for cutting and scoring and to protect your table top.

Waxed paper: You will need this for protection when using super glue.

Baking soda.

IMPORTANT CONSTRUCTION TIPS

Take your time and work carefully, being sure to follow instructions. Use the construction tips that follow to make your model its most efficient and attractive.

CUTTING

Although most of your cutting can be done with scissors, the hobby knife works best when cutting narrow slots.

When cutting out parts, cut in the center of the solid line.

Cut only solid lines. Do not cut dotted or dashed lines.

Before cutting out each part, it is helpful to write the part number on the back of the individual part. **This will allow you to identify the parts once you cut them out.**

Work in numerical order, cutting out only the parts needed for each step before beginning the next step.

SCORING AND BENDING

To make bending along dotted lines easier, first score lightly along the dotted line. You may use the cutting edge of the knife to score, but the easiest way to score is to use the back edge of the cutting blade of your hobby knife. This will prevent the possibility of cutting all the way through the paper. Too much pressure on your knife will cut through the paper. The idea is to cut halfway through the paper. Practice on some scrap paper before working on your model. When the paper bends with a clean open line, you have done the scoring correctly.

Once you have scored the part, lay it over the edge of a table top to make the initial bend. Next, lift the part and continue bending past the 90-degree point. You need to "overbend" the part so that when released it will have a natural tendency to stay at a 90-degree angle.

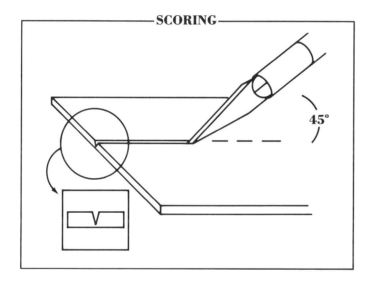

— SCORING —

45°

SCORING AND BENDING RULES: Dashed lines (- - - -) are to be scored **on** printed side of sheet and bent **away** from you. Plus lines (+ + + +) are to be **transferred** to **back** of sheets by using pin holes at each end of the line to be scored and drawing a pencil line on the back of the part between these two points. Score on the pencil line and bend **toward** yourself.

USING PAPER GLUE

Always test for fit before gluing together the parts you have cut out. This gives you a chance to trim if necessary.

Here is the best way to glue with white paper glue: First apply a few drops of glue to one of the two parts to be glued. Spread the glue with a scrap piece of cardboard or paper, leaving only a thin film of glue. Work quickly, since paper absorbs the water in the glue causing it to dry rather fast. Hold the parts being glued together with your hands acting as a clamp. After about one minute, release the parts and check to see if the glue is holding. Apply pressure again if the glue is not yet dry. If the glue doesn't set in one minute, you are probably using too much glue.

USING "SUPER GLUE"

CAUTION: "SUPER GLUES" SHOULD BE HANDLED WITH EXTREME CARE. THEY ARE EXTREMELY DIFFICULT TO REMOVE FROM THE SKIN AND MAY IN FACT BOND SKIN TO SKIN. WHEN APPLYING SUPER GLUE TO A PART, ALWAYS HOLD THE PART BY WRAPPING A PIECE OF WAXED PAPER LOOSELY AROUND IT. THIS WILL HELP KEEP THE SUPER GLUE AWAY FROM YOUR SKIN. APPLY THIS GLUE IN VERY SMALL QUANTITIES TO AVOID SPILLING. READ WARNING ON SUPER GLUE LABEL.

This glue helps make your model functional and long-lasting. It also allows you to sand the paper where instructed without leaving a fuzzy surface. It is used on some holes to form a bearing surface where a metal shaft passes through paper. You will use this glue to bond metal parts to paper as well. **Always rough up the metal somewhat with sandpaper before gluing.**

DRILLING HOLES

Use the #11 X-Acto blade or equivalent to drill holes where instructed. Place the tip at the point where you need a hole. Twist the knife blade in **one direction only** for a nicely rounded hole; do not twist it back and forth. When the tip of the blade comes through the other side of the paper, stop. Turn the paper over and drill from the other side, using the same technique, until the hole is the desired size.

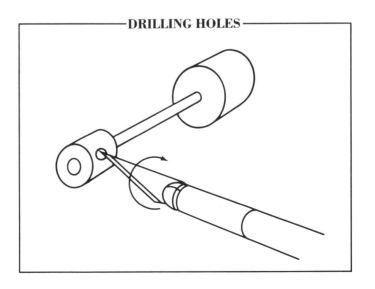

DRILLING HOLES

FORMING CYLINDERS

To form a cylinder from paper it is helpful to pre-bend the paper strip by drawing it across the edge of a counter or table top. Lay the piece of paper on a counter top near the edge. Next, place a book on top of it. Pull the paper across the edge of the counter and down at a 90-degree angle. Once you have pulled it all the way to the end, reverse the ends and repeat the procedure. The paper will now curl naturally.

TABS AND GLUING GUIDES

Tabs are bent and glued to another part to increase the strength of the model. Gluing guides and tabs are areas marked with diagonal lines. They show you where one part will fit onto another and indicate the approximate place where glue should be applied.

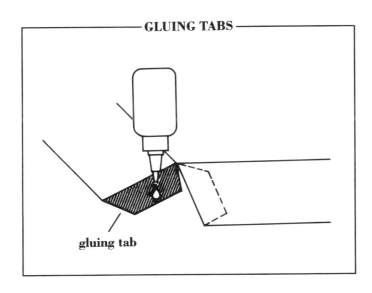

GLUING TABS

gluing tab

THE EXPLODED VIEW

"Exploded" views of the model are provided to guide you in construction. Study the exploded views closely before beginning work and refer to them often while building the model. They will let you see what each part is and will show you how the parts fit together. They are your most important aids for constructing the model.

THE SIDE AND TOP VIEWS

These views are provided to give you a finished-product view.

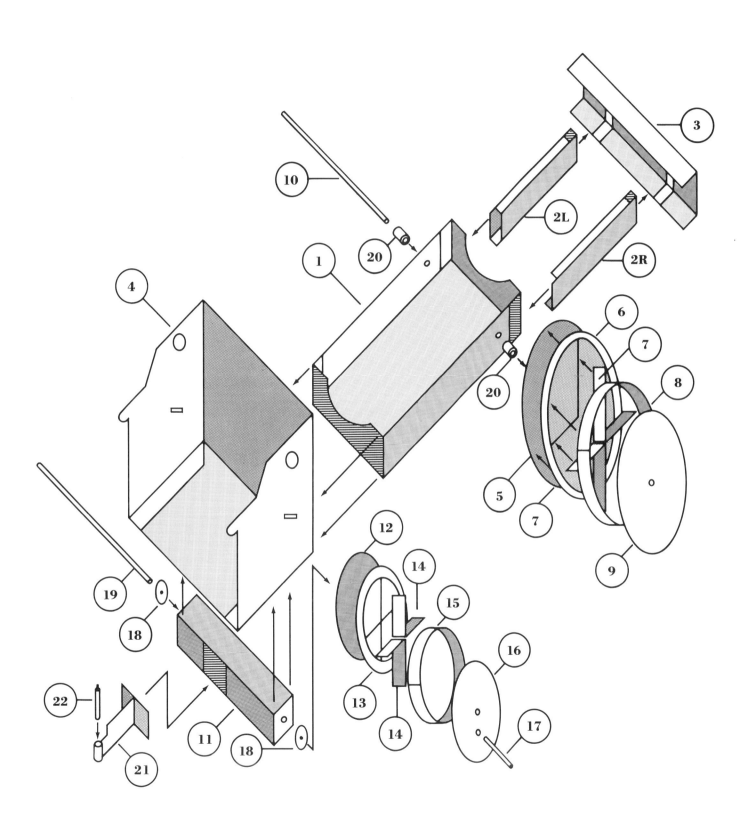

EXPLODED VIEW 2

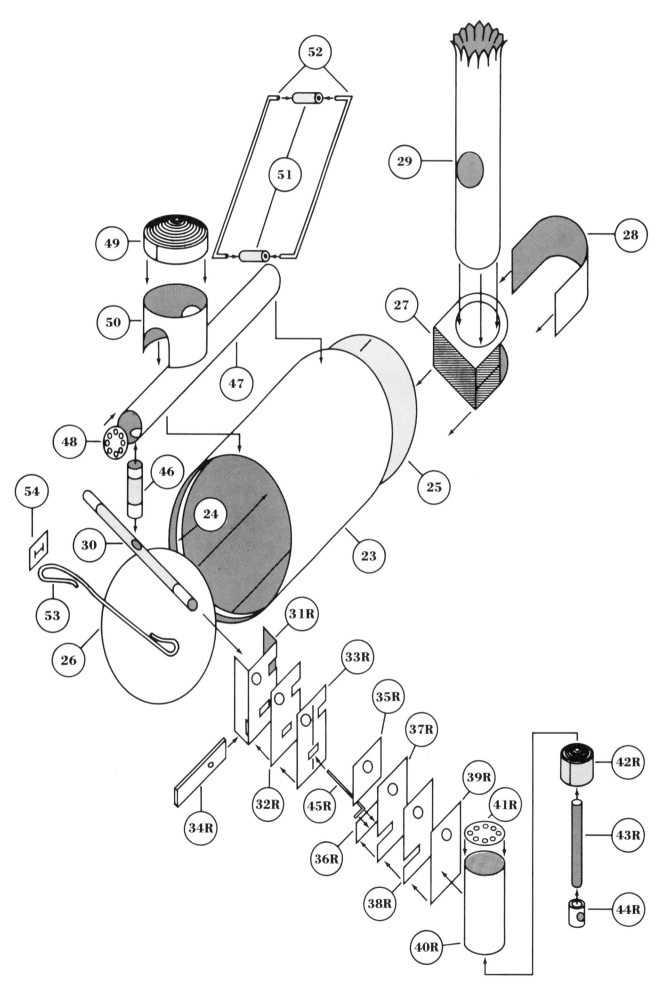

EXPLODED VIEW 3

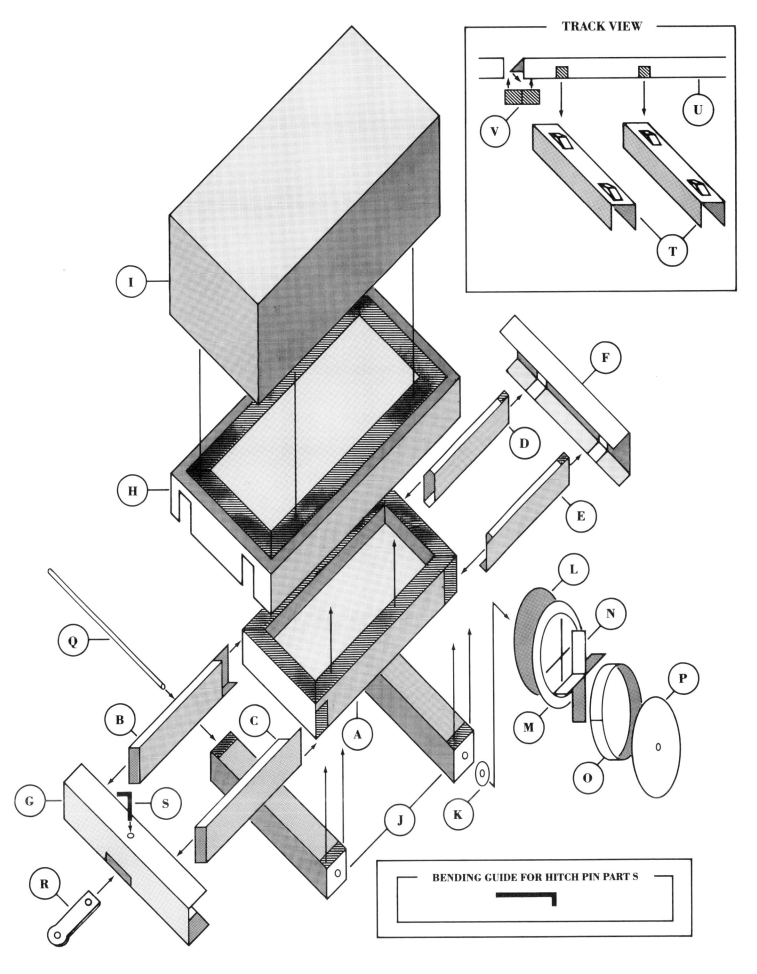

TRACK VIEW

BENDING GUIDE FOR HITCH PIN PART S

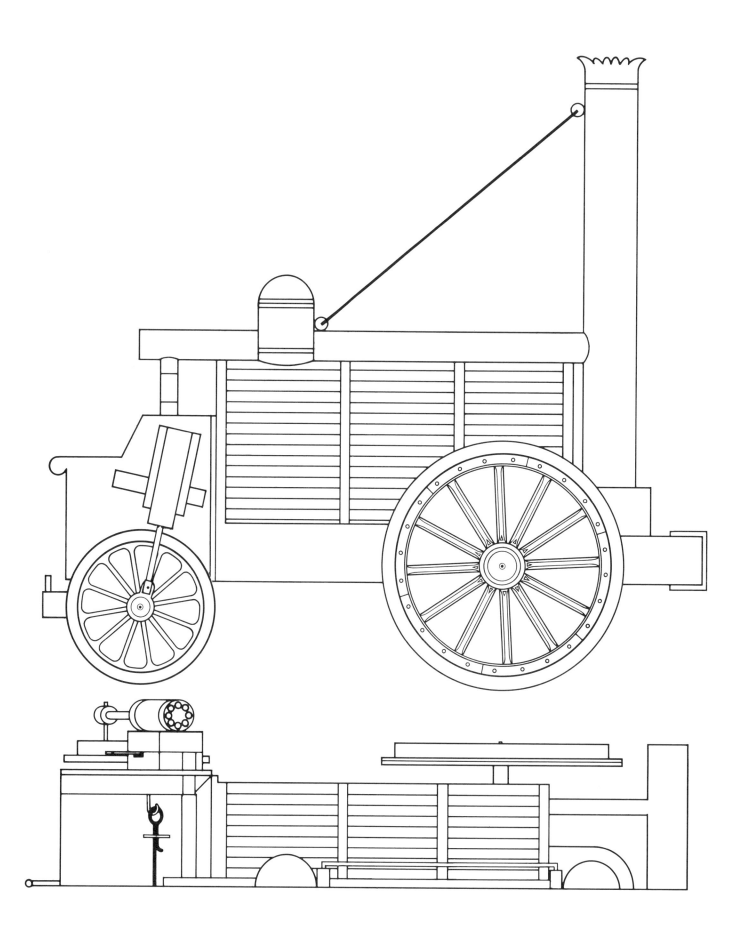

BUILDING
YOUR MODEL

Be sure to read the construction tips and study the exploded views of the model before beginning.

As each step is completed, check the box provided so that you will be better able to keep track of your progress.

Read through the instructions, until you reach a "DO NOW" sign. At that point, stop reading and complete the step just described.

STEP 1: BUILDING THE MAIN FRAME

Preparing the Parts

Cut out parts 1, 2R, 2L, and 3. These parts will become the main frame of your model. DO NOW.

Score and bend part 1 along the dotted lines. Part 1 will have a rectangular shape. Glue with white glue at the tabs and let dry. DO NOW.

Using your hobby knife, or a needle if you prefer, drill holes (indicators provided) in the sides of part 1. The holes should be just large enough to allow a paper-clip wire to pass through. Apply one small drop of super glue to the holes you have just drilled and blow through the hole to keep it clear of glue. The super glue will act as a bearing to reduce wear around the holes you just drilled. DO NOW.

Score and bend parts 2R and 2L. Glue with white glue at tabs and let dry. DO NOW.

Using white glue, glue the notched ends of parts 2R and 2L to part 1. DO NOW.

Score and bend part 3. Apply white glue to the areas folded back-to-back and shape piece to form a bumper. Let dry. DO NOW.

With white glue, glue part 3 to unnotched ends of parts 2R and 2L. DO NOW.

STEP 1

PARTS NEEDED

1   3

2L   2R

TOOLS NEEDED

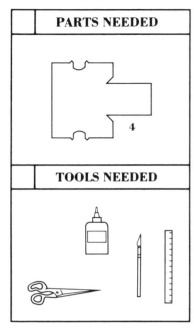

STEP 2: BUILDING THE CAB

Cut out part 4. DO NOW.

Remember scoring and bending rules! Score on **front** of - - - lines, score on **back** of + + + lines.

Score and bend part 4. When you are satisfied with the fit, glue the folds back-to-back using white glue. Let dry. Apply white glue to the two tabs and secure to the floor of part 4. DO NOW.

Using your hobby knife, drill out holes and cut out slots as indicated on part 4. DO NOW.

Glue part 4 to the end of part 1 as shown in exploded view 1. DO NOW.

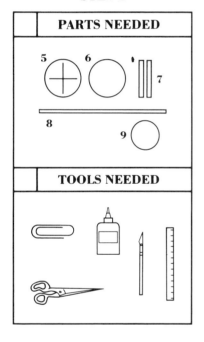

STEP 3: LARGE WHEEL ASSEMBLY

Preparing the Pieces for Assembly

Note: In this step you will assemble 2 large wheels. Assemble one wheel at a time.

Cut out parts 5, 6, 7, 8, and 9. DO NOW.

Glue one part 5 and one part 6 back-to-back and let dry. DO NOW.

Make the outer rim of the wheel from part 8. Pull one part 8 across the edge of a table to form a natural curl. DO NOW.

Make one part 8 into a circle. The ends must overlap just enough to cover the shaded glue area on one end of the part. Use white glue only on the shaded glue area. DO NOW.

Score two of the parts 7 on the dotted line and bend to a 90-degree angle. DO NOW.

In the center of parts 5 and 6, drill a hole just large enough to let a small paper-clip wire pass through. DO NOW.

Place parts 5 and 6 on your work surface with part 6 face up. The lines on part 6 will show you where to glue the parts 7. Using white glue, glue first one part 7 in place and then glue the other. Notice that the lines on part 6 do not touch each other in the center, and neither should the two parts 7. This will leave room for the axle to pass through the wheel. DO NOW.

Refer to exploded view 1 to see how the wheel fits together.

Lay the assembled parts (5, 6, and two 7s) on the work surface and fit the wheel rim (part 8) around the supports (parts 7) and inside of the shaded area provided on part 6. When you are satisfied with the fit, pick up part 8 and apply a small bead of white glue to the edge of the rim all around and replace it onto part 6. DO NOW.

Using your hobby knife, drill a hole in the center of each part 9 just large enough for a small paper-clip wire. DO NOW.

Position part 9 on top of the two parts 7 and inside of the wheel rim (part 8). The wheel rim (part 8) should fit snugly around part 9. Part 9 may need to be trimmed down to achieve this fit. DO NOW.

When satisfied with the fit, remove part 9. If you wish to have your inner and outer spokes match, align before the glue sets. Apply a small bead of glue around the edge of part 9, and another small bead to the edges of the two parts 7. Replace part 9 on top of the two parts 7 and inside of the wheel rim (part 8). Let dry completely. DO NOW.

Repeat the previous instructions to assemble the other large wheel. DO NOW.

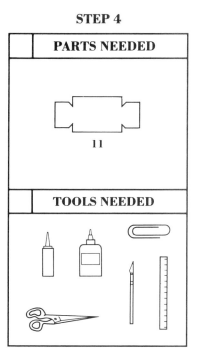

STEP 4: BUILDING THE AXLE BOX

Cut out part 11, the axle box. DO NOW.

Score and bend. Glue up the sides by applying white glue to the glue tabs; let dry completely. DO NOW.

Drill a hole in the ends of the axle box where indicated. The hole should be just large enough to allow a paper-clip wire to pass through. Apply one small drop of super glue to the hole you have just drilled and blow through the hole to keep it clear of glue; this will act as a bearing to reduce wear around the hole. **Be careful not to get super glue on your fingers.** DO NOW.

Part 11 will be glued to the main frame that you built earlier, along the bottom of the cab (part 4).

Apply white glue to the top of part 11. Glue the axle box (part 11) to the gluing guide provided on the bottom of the cab (part 4) and let dry. DO NOW.

STEP 5: SMALL WHEEL ASSEMBLY

Preparing the Pieces for Assembly

Note: In this step you will assemble two small wheels. Assemble one wheel at a time.

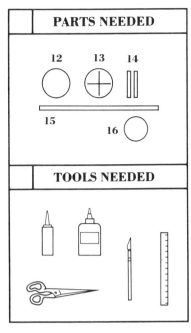

PARTS NEEDED

12   13   14

15

16

TOOLS NEEDED

Cut out parts 12, 13, 14, 15, and 16. DO NOW.

Glue one part 12 and one part 13 back-to-back and let dry. DO NOW.

Part 15 will form the outer rim of the wheel. Pull one part 15 across the edge of a table to form a natural curl. DO NOW.

Make part 15 into a circle. The ends must overlap just enough to cover the shaded area on one end of the part. Use white glue only on the shaded glue area. DO NOW.

Score two of the parts 14 on the dotted line and bend to a 90-degree angle. DO NOW.

In the center of parts 12 and 13, drill a hole just large enough to let a small paper-clip wire pass through. DO NOW.

Place parts 12 and 13 on your work surface with part 13 face up. The lines on part 13 will show you where to glue the two parts 14. Using white glue, glue first one part 14 in place and then the other. Notice that these lines do not touch each other in the center of part 13 and neither should the two parts 14. This will leave room for the axle to pass through the wheel. DO NOW.

Refer to exploded view 1 to see how the wheel fits together.

Lay the assembled parts (12, 13, and two 14s) on the work surface and fit the wheel rim (part 15) around the supports (parts 14) and inside of the shaded area provided on part 13. When you are satisfied with the fit, pick up part 15 and apply a small bead of white glue to the edge of the rim and replace it onto part 13. DO NOW.

Using your hobby knife, drill a hole in the center of part 16 just large enough for a small paper-clip wire. DO NOW.

Next, position part 16 into place on top of the two parts 14 and inside of the wheel rim (part 15). The wheel rim should fit snugly around part 16. DO NOW.

When satisfied with the fit, remove part 16. Apply a small bead of glue around the edge of part 16 and another small bead of glue to the edges of the two parts 14. Replace part 16 on top of the two parts 14 and inside of the wheel rim (part 15). Let dry completely. DO NOW.

Repeat the previous instructions to assemble the other small wheel. DO NOW.

STEP 6: PREPARING AXLES AND CRANK PINS

Refer to the Cutting and Bending guide provided for your assistance.

The axles (part 10 and part 19) are made from paper clips. Straighten out a paper clip until it is as smooth and straight as you can get it. Use your needle-nose pliers if desired, and keep working on it until it is nice and straight. You will need two axles. DO NOW.

When you have the two paper clips straightened to your satisfaction, use the axle length guide provided (for parts 10 and 19) to cut the paper clips to the proper length. DO NOW.

Attaching the Small Wheel Crank Pins

Trim two straight pins to the length provided for part 17 in the Cutting and Bending guide. DO NOW.

There is an indicator on part 16 of the small wheel assembly showing where the crank pin is to be positioned. Position one of the untrimmed straight pins on the indicator and push it through the wheel to the back side. **Important:** Be sure that pin holes line up so that the crank pin is at a 90-degree angle to the wheel. DO NOW.

Remove the straight pin. From the back side of the wheel (part 12), insert a trimmed straight pin (part 17). The head of the pin should just meet part 12. Apply one small drop of super glue to the head of the pin and to the pin shaft on the other side of the wheel. This will secure the crank pin to the wheel to prevent movement. DO NOW.

Repeat the previous instructions for the other small wheel and crank pin. DO NOW.

STEP 7: ATTACHING THE LARGE WHEELS TO THE MAIN FRAME

Refer to exploded view 1.

Cut out the two parts 20. Roll each part 20 into a tight roll to form a small, solid cylinder, leaving a hole in the center large enough to slide the paper-clip axle through. Glue with white glue. DO NOW.

Slide one large wheel onto the end of the axle (part 10). The axle should protrude through the outside of the large wheel just enough to be able to apply one small drop of super glue. Also apply a drop of super glue to the axle on the inside of the wheel. DO NOW.

STEP 6

PARTS NEEDED
10
19
17

TOOLS NEEDED

STEP 7

PARTS NEEDED
20

TOOLS NEEDED

Slide one part 20 onto the axle and glue to the wheel using super glue. DO NOW.

Slide the axle with the large wheel attached through the main frame. Now slide the other part 20 onto the axle on the other side of the main frame. DO NOW.

Slide the other large wheel onto the axle. Glue part 20 to the inside of the large wheel using a small drop of super glue. DO NOW.

The two parts 20 now glued to the large wheels should fit close to the main frame, but not so tight as to restrict the large wheels from spinning freely. When you are satisfied with the fit, apply a drop of super glue to the axle on the outside of the large wheel. DO NOW.

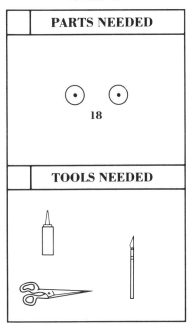

STEP 8

PARTS NEEDED

18

TOOLS NEEDED

STEP 8: ATTACHING THE SMALL WHEELS TO THE MAIN FRAME

Refer to exploded view 1.

Cut out the two parts 18. Slide one part 18 onto the axle (part 19). Slide one of the small wheels onto the axle, with the end of the axle protruding through the small wheel enough to apply a drop of super glue to the end. Apply a drop of super glue here and to the inside of the wheel and axle. DO NOW.

Slide the axle through the holes in the axle box (part 11) of the main frame. Now slide the other part 18 onto axle at the other end of the axle box. DO NOW.

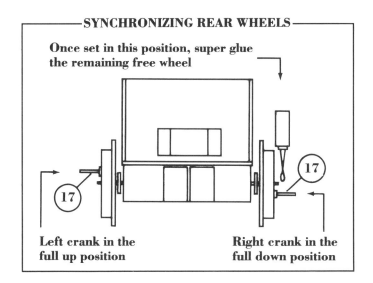

SYNCHRONIZING REAR WHEELS

Once set in this position, super glue the remaining free wheel

17

17

Left crank in the full up position

Right crank in the full down position

Slide the other small wheel onto axle. Position crank pins (parts 17) **opposite** each other per diagram and glue. Apply super glue to outside of small wheel and axle as shown. Give small wheels a spin. They should spin freely and without much friction.

STEP 9: BUILDING THE HITCH

Cut out part 21. Score and bend. DO NOW.

A round toothpick is needed for part 22. Refer to coupler pin (part 22) on the Cutting and Bending guide to find how long to cut the toothpick. DO NOW.

Insert part 22, point up, all the way to the bottom of the scored end of part 21. Using white glue, glue part 22 and all along the inside of part 21. DO NOW.

Using white glue, glue part 21 to indicator shown on axle box (part 11). DO NOW.

STEP 10: BUILDING THE BOILER

Cut out parts 23, 24 (two pieces), 25, and 26. DO NOW.

Use a needle to make a small hole at the places marked with A, B, C, and D on part 23. Three holes will allow you to find these places on the back side of this part when you get to the next step. DO NOW.

Turn part 23 over and use pencil and ruler to draw, on the back side, a line from A to B and a line from C to D. DO NOW.

The two parts 24 are the boiler end-cap supports. They are **not** to be located at the edge of part 23. The two pencil lines you have drawn on the back of part 23 will show how far away from the edge of part 23 (back) you should glue the two parts 24. Using white glue, glue the two parts 24 in place, one at each inside edge of the pencil lines. DO NOW.

Let the glue dry completely before proceeding.

Pull part 23 across the edge of a table to form a natural curl, as explained in the construction tips. Pull vertically, from A to B, not from A to C. DO NOW.

Glue part 23 into a circle to form the boiler; overlap only on the shaded glue area and glue **exactly**, using white glue. (This overlap should make parts 25 and 26 fit perfectly.) DO NOW.

When this glue is **completely dry**, you will find it easy to use your hands to smooth part 23 into a nice round shape. Work slowly and try to get any wrinkles smoothed out so that the boiler will have a nice appearance. DO NOW.

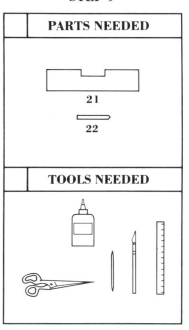

STEP 9

PARTS NEEDED

21

22

TOOLS NEEDED

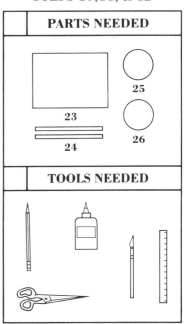

STEPS 10, 11, & 12

PARTS NEEDED

23

24

25

26

TOOLS NEEDED

STEP 11: GLUING THE BOILER ENDS IN PLACE

Put the first boiler end-cap (part 25) into place but do not glue; it should fit snugly and flush into one end of part 23, with the arrow indicators aligned with the outside seam on part 23.

Put the other boiler end-cap (part 26) into place on the other end of the boiler but do not glue. Be sure to align arrow with outside seam on part 23. DO NOW.

When satisfied with the fit of both end-caps, run a bead of white glue around the outside edge of each piece to attach them permanently to the boiler. DO NOW.

Allow glue to dry completely before proceeding.

STEP 12: INSTALLING THE BOILER ON THE MAIN FRAME

Put the boiler you have just built into place on the main frame (part 1) but **do not glue.** When the boiler is properly placed, the arrow on part 1 should line up with the arrow on boiler end-cap (part 26). Pick up the boiler and apply a bead of white glue along the edge of part 1 of the main frame that will hold the boiler. DO NOW.

Replace boiler into part 1 and let dry completely. DO NOW.

STEP 13: BUILDING THE SMOKESTACK BASE

Cut out part 27. Score and bend. DO NOW.

Cut out part 28. This part will wrap around the open end of part 27. Check for fit. When satisfied with fit, apply white glue to glue tabs on part 27. Wrap part 28 around part 27 and clamp your fingers until glue dries. DO NOW.

STEP 14: BUILDING THE SMOKESTACK

Cut out part 29. Pull it across the edge of a table lengthwise to give it a natural curl. DO NOW.

One end of part 29 has a shaded area which will show you how much overlap you need when you roll it into a cylinder shape to form the smokestack. Start with the shaded end of part 29 and carefully match the border. Apply a thin bead of glue and continue rolling to form the cylinder shape. Use white glue at the very end of the final wrap to hold it in place. DO NOW.

Carefully cut out the crown at the top of the smokestack and flair ends out slightly. DO NOW.

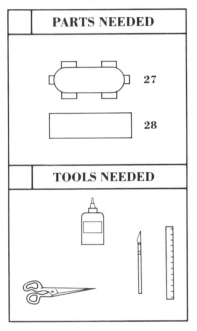

STEP 13

PARTS NEEDED

27

28

TOOLS NEEDED

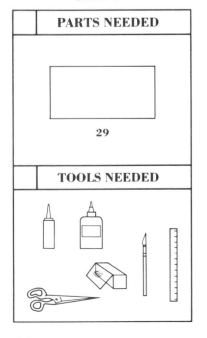

STEP 14

PARTS NEEDED

29

TOOLS NEEDED

Put super glue around the top end (crown) of the smokestack. Apply enough glue to get the paper wet both inside and outside and at least one inch down the side of the smokestack. This will make the top of the smokestack strong and waterproof. DO NOW.

Cut out the hole as indicated on the side of the smokestack using your hobby knife. This hole will eventually hold the air tube (part 47). This hole should be facing the boiler when the smokestack is glued to the base (part 27).

Apply a bead of white glue to the bottom of the smokestack and glue to indicator on smokestack base (part 27). DO NOW.

STEP 15: BUILDING THE AIR TUBE

Cut out part 30 and pull it across the edge of a table to give it a natural curl. DO NOW.

Use a ballpoint-pen refill as a form for making the air tube. Roll part 30 from A to B tightly around the tube of the pen refill. Use white glue on the edge of the last wrap to hold it in place. DO NOW.

When the glue is dry, slide the air tube off the refill tube. Using your hobby knife, drill the hole as indicated through one side of the air tube. Do not drill all the way through the air tube. DO NOW.

Now slide the air tube (part 30) through the holes you drilled in the sides of the cab (part 5). **Do not glue.** DO NOW.

STEP 16: BUILDING THE MAIN VALVE PLATES

Parts 31L and R, 32L and R, and 33L and R will form the main valve plates. The valve plates are important parts of the engine. Instructions must be followed exactly to obtain the best engine performance. NOTICE THE PARTS ARE IDENTIFIED FOR **RIGHT** SIDE AND **LEFT** SIDE. BUILD ONLY ONE SIDE AT A TIME AND KEEP SIDES APART.

Be especially careful not to bend or otherwise deform these valve plates while working on them. **Be extremely careful to keep the super glue off your fingers.**

Cut out part 31R. Use the hobby knife to cut out the pivot pin slot and exhaust slot. Score and bend. Apply white glue to the two glue tabs, glue to sides, and let dry. DO NOW.

Cut out parts 32R and 33R. Cut out the pivot pin slot and the exhaust slot on each piece. DO NOW.

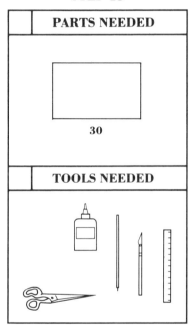

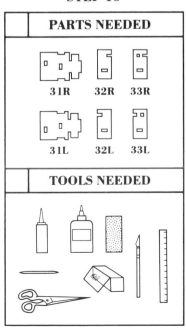

Place a sheet of waxed paper over your work surface. Stack parts 31R, 32R, and 33R together with part 33R on top (line facing up) and part 31R on bottom. When they are lined up exactly, apply a drop of super glue to the edges of the stack at each corner to hold them together while you allow the glue to set. DO NOW.

Gluing the Parts Together

Apply super glue carefully all around the edges of the assembly until the edges are wet. Place the assembly flat on the waxed-paper-covered work surface. Fold the waxed paper over the assembly to protect your fingers and press the **inside** of part 31R firmly with the handle of your hobby knife.

Remove the waxed paper. Apply super glue to the top surface of the assembly. Use another piece of waxed paper to protect your fingers and turn the assembly top down and rub on the waxed paper to spread the glue around. This is done to make sure the glue completely covers, and helps smooth, the surface. Put the assembly aside until the glue has completely set. DO NOW.

When the glue is completely dry, hold the valve plate face up and use the hobby knife to drill the intake hole. It is important that the intake hole is the right size. It should be just large enough to allow a round toothpick to pass through. DO NOW.

After drilling the intake hole, apply a small amount of super glue around the hole. This will stiffen the paper and allow you to shave away the ridge of paper formed around the hole by the drilling opertion. Shave away the ridge when the glue has set. DO NOW.

Place a piece of sandpaper on a flat surface and place the face of the valve plate assembly flat on the piece of sandpaper. Sand lightly to remove any rough spots. **Be careful not to bend the valve plate or round off the edges while sanding.** DO NOW.

Now repeat the previous procedures to build the Left Main Valve Plate. DO NOW.

STEP 17: INSTALLING THE MAIN VALVE PLATES

The main valve plates just completed will be glued onto part 4. Their locations are shown by the white rectangular glue areas on the sides of part 4. It is very important that these plates are glued onto part 4 correctly. **Do not glue yet.**

Notice that the slots you cut in part 4 should line up with the slots you cut in the main valve plates. The air tube (part 30) and the air intake holes in the main valve plates should also line up. Each end of the air tube (part 30) will fit flush to the inside of and around the air intake holes on each main valve plate. To ensure that the air intake holes are aligned with the air tube holes, you should insert a toothpick into the holes. **Be sure that the hole you drilled earlier in the air tube is facing straight up.** DO NOW.

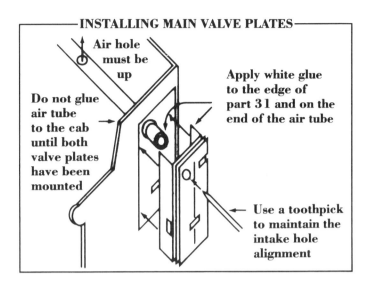

When you are satisfied with the fit, apply a bead of white glue to the edge of one main valve plate and around the end of the air tube (part 30). Attach to part 4 and hold tight until the glue sets. **Let dry completely.** DO NOW.

Now glue the other main valve plate to part 4. Be certain of proper alignment. **Let dry completely.** DO NOW.

It is important that there is a good seal between the ends of the air tube and the air intake holes to ensure against air leaks. If there is an air leak, coat the joint with white glue.

Apply a bead of white glue around air tube where it passes through the sides of the cab (part 4). This will secure the air tube to the cab. DO NOW.

STEP 18: BUILDING THE CYLINDER VALVE PLATES

Parts 35, 36, 37, 38, and 39 left (L) and right (R) will form the cylinder valve plates. **Notice the parts are identified for RIGHT side and LEFT side. Build only one side at a time and keep sides apart.**

Cut out parts 35R, 36R, 37R, 38R, and 39R. Cut out the slots on parts 37R and 38R. DO NOW.

Stack parts 37R, 38R, and 39R together with part 37R on top and part 39R on the bottom. Line them up carefully and apply a drop of super glue to the edge at the four corners. When this glue has set, place the assembly flat on a

STEP 18

PARTS NEEDED			
36R	37R	38R	39R
35R			
36L	37L	38L	39L
35L			

TOOLS NEEDED

piece of waxed paper and apply super glue all around the edges. Fold the waxed paper over the part to protect your fingers and press down to keep the assembly flat while the glue sets. DO NOW.

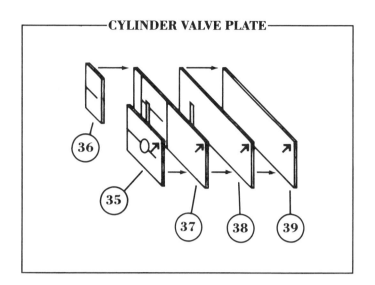

CYLINDER VALVE PLATE

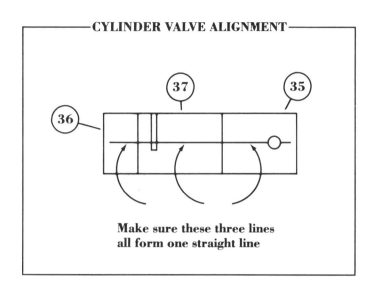

CYLINDER VALVE ALIGNMENT

Make sure these three lines
all form one straight line

Refer to the diagrams and glue parts 35R and 36R in place using **white** glue. The correct placement of parts 35R and 36R on part 37R is important. The markings on parts 35R, 36R, and 37R will help you line up the parts correctly. Study the diagrams carefully. DO NOW.

When parts 35R and 36R are in place and the glue has completely set, apply several drops of super glue to their front surfaces, turn them face down on waxed paper, and rub to spread the glue around. Remove from the waxed paper and let it dry to leave a smooth surface. DO NOW.

When the glue has completely set, put the assembly face down on a piece of fine sandpaper and sand lightly to get a smooth surface. DO NOW.

Next, drill the intake hole shown on part 35R. Drill the hole large enough to pass a round toothpick through it. DO NOW.

Put a drop of super glue in the hole but make sure that excess glue does not block the hole. Shave away the ridge left by the drilling process, then sand lightly by placing the part face down on a piece of fine sandpaper laid flat on a table. DO NOW.

Finally, use the knife blade to clean out the hole to toothpick size. DO NOW.

Now repeat the previous instructions to build the Left Cylinder Valve Plate. DO NOW.

STEP 19: BUILDING THE ENGINE CYLINDERS

Parts 40 and 41 will form the engine cylinders. Once again, you are building cylinders for a right side and a left side. **Build one side at a time and keep sides apart.**

Preparing the Parts

Cut out parts 40R and 41R. DO NOW.

Place part 40R face up on waxed paper and apply several drops of super glue to the shaded glue area. Fold the waxed paper over the part and rub so that the super glue is spread evenly and completely saturates this area. Remove waxed paper and let glue set. DO NOW.

When the super glue has set, sand both sides of this area lightly to leave a smooth surface. DO NOW.

Forming the Engine Cylinder

First, pull part 40R across the edge of a table lengthwise several times to give it a natural curl. DO NOW.

Wrap part 40R around the handle of your hobby knife (or a ⁵⁄₁₆″ shaft) to form the cylinder. Begin with the glued end of part 40R and wrap toward the dotted end. Keep the wraps tight and even. When the wraps are complete, use white glue on the end of the last wrap to hold it in place. Refer to diagram. DO NOW.

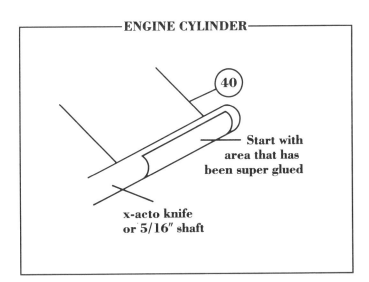

ENGINE CYLINDER

40

Start with area that has been super glued

x-acto knife or 5/16″ shaft

When this glue is dry, carefully slide the cylinder until it is halfway off the end of the knife handle. Now apply a few drops of super glue to the outside of the cylinder and use a small piece of waxed paper to spread the glue all around the outside of the cylinder to wet the entire surface. **Be extremely careful not to allow the super glue to come into contact with the knife handle. Otherwise you will be unable to remove the cylinder without distorting its shape.** DO NOW.

When the glue is completely set, carefully remove the cylinder from the knife handle. DO NOW.

Using white glue, glue the cylinder end-cap (part 41R) onto the end of the cylinder, as indicated on part 40R, using white glue. DO NOW.

When the glue is dry, blow gently into the open end to check for air leaks. If a leak is found, plug with white glue or apply baking soda to the area, dust lightly with a Q-Tip, then apply super glue. DO NOW.

Apply a small amount of super glue around the edge of the open end of the cylinder to stiffen it. This will also form a small ridge just inside the cylinder opening. Use the knife blade to very gently scrape away this ridge once the glue has set. DO NOW.

Handle the cylinder carefully so as not to deform it when working on it. Drill the intake hole at the proper point on the cylinder. The hole should be just large enough to allow a round toothpick to pass through it. DO NOW.

Now repeat the previous instructions to build the Left Engine Cylinder. DO NOW.

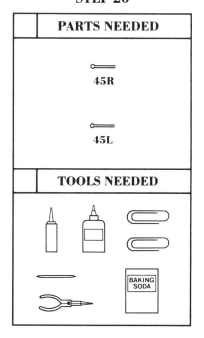

STEP 20: ATTACHING THE CYLINDER VALVE PLATE TO THE CYLINDER

Work with one side at a time.

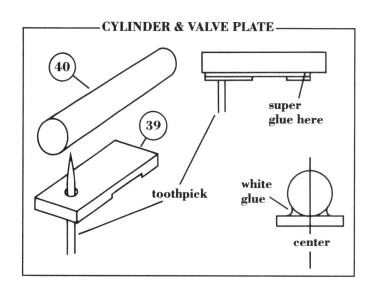

Refer to the Cylinder and Valve Plate diagram for placement of the cylinder valve plate on the cylinder. To line them up, use a toothpick pushed through the intake hole in the right cylinder valve plate and then into the intake hole in the right cylinder. The bottom (part 39) of the valve plate should face the cylinder (part 40). To glue the valve plate onto the cylinder, first apply two drops of super glue to the cylinder where the parts will touch and away from the toothpick. Hold the parts together until the glue sets while keeping them lined up as in the diagram. DO NOW.

When the glue has set, gently remove the toothpick. DO NOW.

Check the parts to see if they are lined up properly. If they are, use the end of a toothpick to apply white glue all around the area where the cylinder and the valve plate touch. **Let this glue dry completely before handling, the cylinder assembly again.** DO NOW.

Now attach the left cylinder to the valve plate. DO NOW.

Attaching the Cylinder Pivot Pins

Cut and bend two paper clips to form parts 45R and 45L, the cylinder pivot pins. Use the Cutting and Bending guide provided. DO NOW.

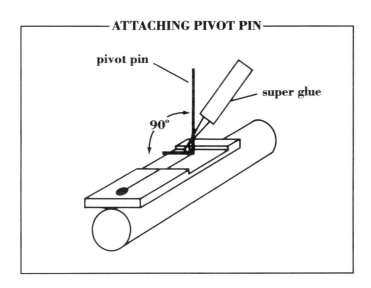

Working on one side at a time, glue the pivot pin onto the cylinder valve plate using super glue, as shown in the accompanying diagram. The short end of the pin fits into the slot in the cylinder valve plate. Dust with baking soda to help fill around the pin, then reapply super glue. **Be careful not to get glue on the flat surface of the valve plate.** DO NOW.

STEP 21: BUILDING THE PISTON AND PISTON ROD

Preparing the Parts

Notice the parts are identified for RIGHT side and LEFT side. Build only one side at a time and keep sides apart.

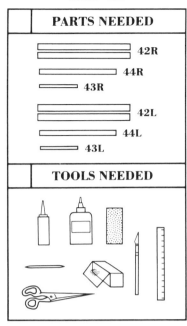

PARTS NEEDED

42R

44R

43R

42L

44L

43L

TOOLS NEEDED

Cut out parts 42R (two pieces) and 44R. DO NOW.

Make part 43R from a round toothpick using the cutting guide provided. DO NOW.

Pull the two pieces of part 42R across the edge of a table to give them a natural curl. DO NOW.

Building the Piston

Wrap one narrow end of the parts 42R around the end of the toothpick to begin forming the piston. Keep the wraps as tight and as even as possible. Use white glue to hold the last wrap in place. DO NOW.

Continue by wrapping the second piece of part 42R **on top** of the first piece where it stopped, allowing no overlap. Check the size of the piston as you wrap this piece, stopping the wrap when a slightly loose fit inside the cylinder (part 40R) has been attained. You will probably use all of the wrap of part 42R, but if you don't, cut off the unused part of piece 42R and apply a very small amount of white glue to temporarily hold it in place. DO NOW.

Check the fit of the piston in the cylinder. It should be a loose fit so that the piston will drop **freely** to the bottom of the cylinder. If necessary, add or remove **one wrap** at a time until a good fit is achieved. DO NOW.

Wrap part 44R around the opposite end of the toothpick to form what will look like a small piston. Glue the final wrap with white glue. DO NOW.

Apply super glue to each end of the piston, at all edges of the paper, and around the outside surfaces so that all paper parts are wet. Use a scrap of waxed paper to wipe away excess glue and leave a smooth surface. DO NOW.

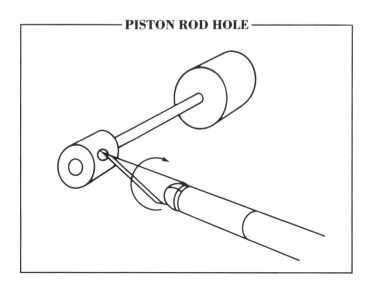

PISTON ROD HOLE

When the super glue has completely set, hold the piston assembly at the middle, wrap a small piece of fine sandpaper around the piston (part 42R), and rotate the piston to smooth and polish it. Check the fit of the piston in the cylinder again and continue to polish with sandpaper if necessary until the piston moves freely in the cylinder. DO NOW.

Use the hobby knife to drill a hole in the small end (part 44R) of the piston rod. Drill first one side and then the other. Make the hole large enough for the crank pin (part 17) to pass freely through it. The hole should go right through the paper and the wood. Refer to the diagram. DO NOW.

Repeat the previous instructions to build the Left Piston and Piston Rod. DO NOW.

STEP 22: BUILDING THE AIR TUBE

Cut out part 46 and pull it across the edge of a table to give it a natural curl. DO NOW.

Use a ballpoint-pen refill as a form for making the air tube. Roll part 46 tightly around the tube of the pen refill. Use white glue on the edge of the last wrap to hold it in place. DO NOW.

When the glue is dry, slide the air tube off the pen refill tube and set aside. DO NOW.

STEP 23: BUILDING THE AIR TUBE

Cut out part 47. DO NOW.

To form the air tube, place part 47 face down on the work surface. Begin wrapping tightly around the handle of your hobby knife (or a ⁵⁄₁₆″ shaft). Begin with blank end and be sure to keep wraps tight and even. When the wraps are complete, use white glue on the end of the last wrap to hold it in place. DO NOW.

Using your hobby knife, drill the hole in part 47 where indicated. This hole should be just large enough to hold part 46 snugly. DO NOW.

Cut out the end-cap (part 48). Refer to exploded view 2. Apply a bead of white glue to the end of part 47 nearest to the hole you just drilled. Attach part 48 and let dry completely. DO NOW.

When the glue is dry, blow gently into the open end to check for air leaks. If a leak is found, plug with white glue or apply baking soda to the area, dust lightly with a Q-Tip, then apply super glue. DO NOW.

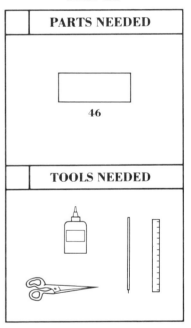

STEP 22

PARTS NEEDED
46

TOOLS NEEDED

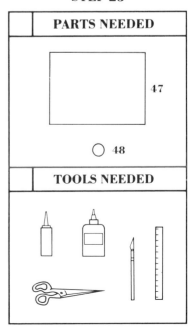

STEP 23

PARTS NEEDED
47
○ 48

TOOLS NEEDED

STEP 24: INSTALLING THE AIR TUBES

Slide part 46 into the hole you drilled in part 47. **Do not glue.** DO NOW.

Slide the other end of part 47 into the hole in the smokestack (part 29). **Do not glue.** DO NOW.

The air tube (part 47) should fit flush on top of the boiler. Part 46 should fit directly on top of the hole in the air tube (part 30).

When you are satisfied with the fit, apply a **small** bead of white glue to the bottom end of part 46. **This is a very close and tight fit. Be sure not to let excess glue plug the holes of the two air tubes (parts 46 and 30). Let dry completely.** DO NOW.

To secure parts 46 and 47 together, put white glue around the hole in part 47 and around the shaft of part 46. DO NOW.

Secure parts 29 and 47 together by applying white glue around the hole in part 29 and around the shaft of the air tube (part 47). DO NOW.

Secure the air tube (part 47) to the boiler by running a small bead of white glue along the area where the air tube and the boiler touch. **Let dry.** DO NOW.

When all the glue is dry you may check for air leaks in the air tubes by covering the intake holes on parts 33R and 33L with your fingers and gently blowing into the smokestack. If no air escapes, you have properly sealed all the connections. If a leak is found, plug with white glue or apply baking soda to the area, dust lightly with a Q-Tip, then apply super glue.

STEP 25: BUILDING THE STEAM DOME

Cut out part 49. Cut out each of the eight strips. Using white glue, glue the strips end-to-end making about a ¼″ overlap on each strip. This will give you one long strip of paper. DO NOW.

Begin at one end of the long strip of paper. Tuck the end over and begin rolling the strip into a round disc shape. Keep the wraps as tight and even as possible. Use white glue to hold the last wrap in place. **Let dry completely.** DO NOW.

Gently push on the center of the strips that you have just wrapped together to form a dome shape, referring to the side view for guidance. DO NOW.

Once you have shaped the dome to your satisfaction, apply super glue to wet the entire dome. Let dry. DO NOW.

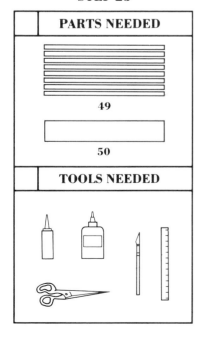

STEP 25

PARTS NEEDED

49

50

TOOLS NEEDED

Cut out part 50, which will form the base for your steam dome. Attach the blank end of part 50 flush to the end of the last wrap on the dome you have just built. Wrap part 50 around the dome until only the printed portion is left showing. Use white glue to hold the last wrap in place. DO NOW.

Refer to the side view for placement of steam dome. Use your hobby knife to cut out a portion of each side of the steam dome which will enable you to slide it over the air tube (part 47) and onto the boiler. It should be placed in the center of the striped area of part 47. DO NOW.

When you are satisfied with the fit, apply white glue to the bottom edge of the steam dome and attach, with the air tube, to the boiler. **Let dry.** DO NOW.

STEP 26: BUILDING THE SMOKESTACK SUPPORT RODS

Cut out the two parts 51. Wrap one of the parts 51 around the end of a straightened paper clip. Keep the wraps as tight and even as possible. Use white glue to hold the last wrap in place. DO NOW.

When the glue is dry slide part 51 off of the paper clip. Wrap the other part 51 as you did the first. DO NOW.

You will need two paper clips to form parts 52. Bend and form support rods per the Cutting and Bending guide for part 52. DO NOW.

Refer to exploded view 2. Apply a drop of super glue to the ends of the parts 52 and insert into the ends of parts 51. **Let dry.** DO NOW.

Refer to the side view for placement of smokestack support rods. Apply a drop of white glue to each end of the assembled support rods and attach one end to the steam dome and air tube. Attach the other end of the support rods to an appropriate location on the smokestack. **Let dry completely.** DO NOW.

STEP 27: BUILDING THE ADJUSTING TABS

Cut out parts 34R and 34L. Score, bend each part back-to-back, and glue each part 34 with white glue. DO NOW.

Drill a hole large enough to fit a small paper-clip wire at the place indicated by a dot on each part 34. Apply one drop of super glue on the hole, and blow to clear the hole of excess super glue. This will act as a bearing. DO NOW.

Slide part 34R into the slot in the side of the right main valve plate (part 31R) per exploded view 2. **Do not glue.** DO NOW.

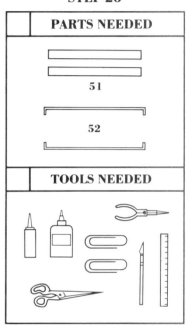

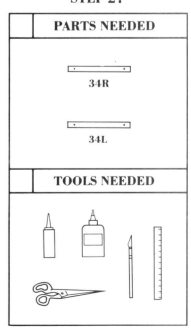

Slide part 34L into the slot in the side of the left main valve plate (part 31L). **Do not glue.** DO NOW.

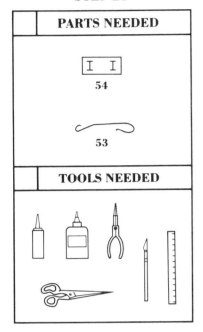

STEP 28

PARTS NEEDED
I I
54
〰
53

TOOLS NEEDED

STEP 28: INSTALLING THE CYLINDER ASSEMBLIES

Part 53, which is made from a rubber band, acts as a valve spring to hold the cylinder valve plates against the main valve plates.

Cut out part 54. Score and bend. Glue back-to-back using white glue. DO NOW.

Part 54 is the tension adjuster for the rubber band (part 53). Slide a looped (but not glued or tied) end of part 53 through the H slot in the center of part 54. DO NOW.

Make a small loop out of the other end of the rubber band and apply a small drop of super glue to hold the loop. DO NOW.

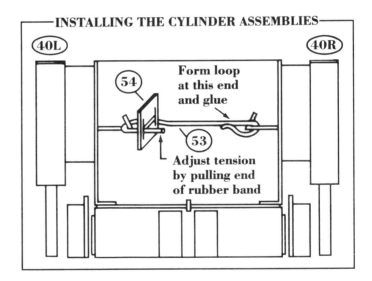

INSTALLING THE CYLINDER ASSEMBLIES

Refer to the diagram. Slide the right cylinder assembly pivot pin (part 45R) through the slot in the right main valve plate, through the hole in the adjusting tab (part 34R), and match the main valve plate and the cylinder assembly together. DO NOW.

Very carefully use your needle-nose pliers to bend the end of the right pivot pin up to a little more than a 90-degree angle. This bend will enable you to slip the looped end of the rubber band (part 53) onto the pivot pin. DO NOW.

Now slide the left cylinder assembly pivot pin through the slot in the left main valve plate, through the hole in the adjusting tab, and match the main valve plate and the cylinder assembly together. DO NOW.

Very carefully use your needle-nose pliers to bend the end of the left pivot pin up to a little more than a 90-degree angle. This bend will enable you to slip the looped end of the rubber band with part 54, the tension adjuster, onto the pivot pin. DO NOW.

The rubber band (part 53) should be very loose in order to allow the engine to run properly. Work carefully to get it just tight enough to keep the cylinder valve plates against the main valve plates.

STEP 29: INSTALLING THE PISTONS

Install the large pistons (parts 42R and 42L) into the cylinders (parts 40R and 40L) and slide the crank pins (parts 17) through the hole in the small end of the piston rod (part 44R and 44L). DO NOW.

STEP 30: BUILDING THE BALLOON HOLDER

Use parts 55 and 56 to make the balloon holder. It will serve as a nozzle which will fit into the open end of the smokestack and will hold the balloon, which will provide the air pressure to make your "steamless" steamer run.

Cut out part 55 and pull it across the edge of a table to give it a natural curl. DO NOW.

Roll part 55 into a tube. It should form a tapered tube that will fit snugly partway into the open end of the smokestack (tapered end first). Glue the last wrap with white glue. DO NOW.

Cut out the three parts 56. DO NOW.

Roll one part 56 around part 55 to form a reinforcing band at the stripe on part 55. Glue the last wrap with white glue. Attach the next part 56 on the indicated overlap and continue wrapping. Glue the last wrap with white glue. Add the final part 56 in the same way, gluing the final wrap. DO NOW.

Check the fit of the balloon holder you just made. It should fit snugly into the smokestack. DO NOW.

Use a piece of waxed paper wrapped loosely around the balloon holder to hold it while you apply super glue. Work carefully to make sure the super glue does not come into contact with your hands. Apply enough super glue to wet all parts of the balloon holder both inside and outside, and including the reinforcing band. DO NOW.

STEP 30

PARTS NEEDED
55
56

TOOLS NEEDED

TESTING YOUR STEAMLESS STEAMER

Check the exploded views and the boxes beside each step in the instructions to make sure all parts are assembled correctly. When you are satisfied, it is time for a test run.

First apply a small amount of graphite powder into the open end of the engine cylinders and between the valve plates. This will lubricate the engines for smoother running.

Check the alignment of the inlet hole in the main valve plate with the inlet hole in the cylinder valve plate on each side according to the diagram in the instructions. Adjust the pivot pin adjusting tabs (parts 34) as necessary to get proper alignment. Parts 34 are **timing devices;** moving these tabs very slowly up and down will compensate for any minor misalignment. This must be performed while the engines are running.

Use two balloons to power your steamless steamer. Put one balloon inside another. Install the balloons on the balloon holder, pulling the open end down over the reinforcing band so that it will stay on. Blow up the balloon and use the first two fingers (not the thumb) to pinch the neck of the balloon while you insert the balloon holder into the smokestack.

Release the balloon and turn one of the small wheels very gently to start the engines running. The engines should run for several seconds.

Do not be disappointed if the locomotive does not run on the first attempt. There are several things to check and several adjustments you can make to get your engines running or to improve the way they run. Read **Troubleshooting and Tuning Your Engines** to determine what adjustments to make.

TROUBLESHOOTING AND TUNING YOUR ENGINES

If your engines do not run on the first attempt, the following suggestions may solve your problem.

1. Some balloons are unusually weak. You can find out if this is your problem by simply blowing directly into the smokestack. If the engines run after turning one of the small wheels gently, then you have been using weak balloons. Nine-inch latex balloons are best. Remember that it is usually necessary to give one of the small wheels a gentle spin to start the engines.

2. Check the tension of the valve spring (rubber band). It should be just tight enough to keep the cylinder valve plates in **light** contact with the main valve plates. Try reducing the tension. You will probably think it is too loose when it is correctly adjusted.

3. Check the surfaces of the main valve plates and the cylinder valve plates to see if they are smooth. A raised area around the inlet holes caused by drilling or a drop of glue spilled on these surfaces can prevent the engine from running well. If they are not smooth, the best way to correct the problem is as follows:

    With the cylinder still in place, slip a piece of fine sandpaper between the two valve plates. Work the sandpaper back and forth while holding the two valve plates lightly together. Reverse the sandpaper and repeat the procedure. Check the surfaces again and if they are smooth, blow away the dust that remains and apply more graphite powder.

4. Check the air tubes for leaks. Plug the leaks with white glue. Check the air tubes and the inlet holes in the valve plates to make sure they are not blocked.

5. Check the fit of the pistons in the cylinders. They should drop freely to the bottom of the cylinders when released. Also check to see that the cylinders have not been deformed or otherwise damaged. Try inserting the handle of the hobby knife into the cylinders to make sure that they are still round.

6. Check the small wheels for freedom of movement. Make sure that they are not rubbing against another part. The wheels should turn freely and spin several times when given a very gentle push by hand. Remember that too much tension on the rubber band or rough and uneven valve plates will also keep the wheels from spinning freely.

7. It is possible that after running your locomotive numerous times, the moisture from your breath will begin to accumulate in the engines. This

can cause the engines to run poorly. If this happens, simply set the locomotive aside. It will run well again when it has had a short time to dry out.

Do not use the same balloons day after day. This suggestion is made for health considerations and because, after numerous inflations, the balloons will tend to weaken.

BUILDING THE TENDER BOX

The coal car or tender box was crucial to the working functions of each individual locomotive. The tender box carried the extra supply of coal needed to provide the heat to produce steam. It also carried a supply of water for the locomotive. If additional space was available, the tender box could also be used to carry tools, freight, or any other items that needed to be transported.

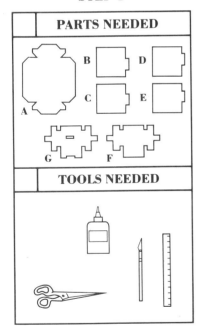

STEP 1: BUILDING THE MAIN FRAME

Preparing the Parts

Cut out part A. Score and bend. Part A will have a rectangular shape. Glue with white glue at tabs and let dry. DO NOW.

Cut out parts B, C, D, and E. Score and bend. Glue each part with white glue at tabs and let dry. DO NOW.

Refer to exploded view 3. Glue the notched ends of parts B, C, D, and E to the indicators on part A, using white glue, and let dry. DO NOW.

Cut out part F. Score and bend. Apply white glue to the areas folded back-to-back and shape part F to form the bumper. Let dry. DO NOW.

Glue part F and the unnotched ends of parts D and E together with white glue. DO NOW.

Cut out part G. Using your hobby knife, cut out the slot in this bumper. Score and bend. Apply white glue to the areas folded back-to-back and shape part G to form the bumper. Let dry. Drill the two holes indicated by a dot on the top and on the bottom of the bumper. These holes should be just large enough to allow a paper-clip wire to pass through. DO NOW.

Glue part G and the unnotched ends of parts B and C together. DO NOW.

STEP 2: BUILDING THE AXLE BOXES

Cut out the two parts J. DO NOW.

Score and bend. Glue up with white glue at the glue tabs and let dry completely. DO NOW.

Drill a hole just large enough to allow a paper-clip wire to pass through in the ends of the axle boxes where indicated. Apply a small drop of super glue to each hole. The drop of super glue will act as a bearing to reduce wear around the holes you have just drilled. DO NOW.

Apply white glue to the top of the axle boxes and glue to the indicators provided on the bottom of parts B, C, D, and E of the main frame. DO NOW.

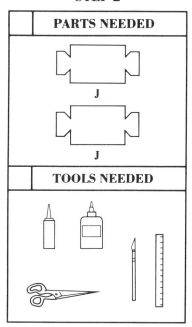

STEP 3: BUILDING THE WHEEL ASSEMBLY

Preparing the Pieces for Assembly

Note: There will be enough parts to assemble four small wheels. Assemble one wheel at a time.

Cut out parts L, M, N, O, and P. DO NOW.

Glue parts L and M back-to-back and let dry. DO NOW.

Make the outer rim of the wheel from part O. Pull one part O across the edge of a table to form a natural curl. DO NOW.

Make part O into a circle, overlapping the ends just enough to cover the shaded area on one end. Use white glue only on the shaded glue area. DO NOW.

You now need two of the parts N provided. Score each on the dotted line and bend to a 90-degree angle. DO NOW.

Drill a hole in the center of parts L and M. Make this hole just large enough to let a small paper-clip wire pass through. DO NOW.

Place parts L and M on your work surface with part M face up. Glue first one part N and then the other in place using white glue; the lines on part M will show you where to glue these parts. Notice that these lines do not touch each other in the center of part M and neither should the two parts N. This will leave room for the axle to pass through the wheel. DO NOW.

Refer to exploded view 3 to see how the wheel fits together.

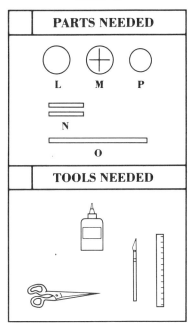

Lay the assembled parts (L, M, and two Ns) on the work surface and fit the wheel rim (part O) around the supports (parts N) and inside of the shaded area provided on part M. When you are satisfied with the fit, pick up part O and apply a small bead of white glue to the edge of the rim and replace it onto part M. DO NOW.

Using your hobby knife, drill a hole in the center of part P just large enough for a small paper-clip wire. DO NOW.

Next, position part P into place on top of the two parts N and inside of the wheel rim (part O). The wheel rim (part O) should fit snugly around part P. DO NOW.

When satisfied with the fit, remove part P and apply a small bead of white glue around the edge of part P. Also apply a small bead of white glue to the edges of the two parts N. Replace part P on top of the two parts N and inside of the wheel rim (part O). Let dry completely. DO NOW.

Repeat the previous instructions to assemble the other small wheels. DO NOW.

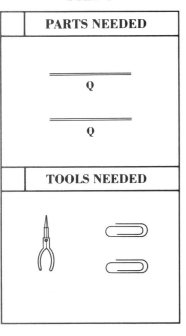

STEP 4: BUILDING THE AXLES

Refer to the Cutting and Bending guide for assistance.

The axles (parts Q) are made from paper clips. Straighten out a paper clip until it is as smooth and straight as you can get it. Use your needle-nose pliers if desired, and keep working on it until it is nice and straight. You will need two axles. DO NOW.

When you have the two paper clips straightened to your satisfaction, use the axle-length guide provided and cut the paper clips to the proper length. DO NOW.

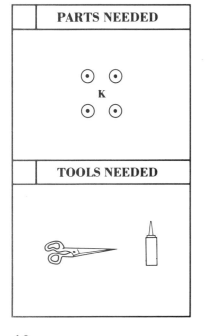

STEP 5: ATTACHING THE WHEELS TO THE MAIN FRAME

Slide one small wheel onto the end of the axle (part Q). The axle should protrude through the outside of the wheel just enough to be able to apply one small drop of super glue. Also apply a drop of super glue to the axle on the inside of the wheel. DO NOW.

Cut out the four parts K. These parts are the wheel washers. DO NOW.

Slide one part K onto the axle with the wheel. Slide the axle through the axle box. DO NOW.

Now slide another part K onto the axle at the other side of the axle box. Slide another wheel onto the end of the axle. The axle should protrude through the outside of the wheel just enough to be able to apply one drop of super glue to the axle. DO NOW.

Repeat the previous instructions to attach the other two wheels and axle to the main frame. DO NOW.

STEP 6: BUILDING THE BOX

Cut out part H. Score and bend. Glue sides with white glue on the tabs and let dry. DO NOW.

Position part H over the top of part A of the main frame. The notches provided in part H will enable you to slide part H on the main frame and position it an equal distance from each bumper. DO NOW.

When you are satisfied with the positioning of part H on the main frame, pick up part H again. Apply white glue to the glue indicators provided on the top of part A. Replace part H in the proper position and let dry. DO NOW.

Cut out part I. Score and bend. Glue sides with white glue on tabs and let dry. DO NOW.

Position part I on top of part H. When you are satisfied with the fit, pick up part I and apply white glue to the glue indicators on part H. Replace part I on top of part H and let dry. DO NOW.

STEP 7: BUILDING THE HITCH

Cut out part R. Score, bend, and glue back-to-back using white glue. DO NOW.

Drill the two holes as indicated by dots on part R, using your hobby knife. The hole at the round end of part R should be just large enough to slide a round toothpick through. The hole at the square end of part R should be just large enough to slide a paper-clip wire through. DO NOW.

Refer to exploded view 3 for bending guide for hitch pin (part S). Use a paper clip to make part S. Cut and bend per the Cutting and Bending guide. DO NOW.

Slide part R into the slot in the bumper part G. DO NOW.

Insert part S through the hole in the top of the bumper (part G), through the hole in the hitch (part R), and into the hole on the bottom of the bumper (part

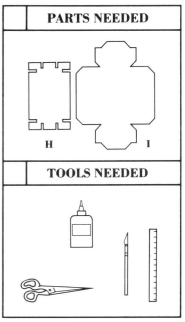

STEP 6

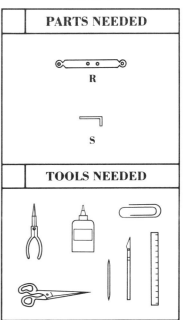

STEP 7

G). This will hold the hitch in place and enable you to attach the tender box to the locomotive. DO NOW.

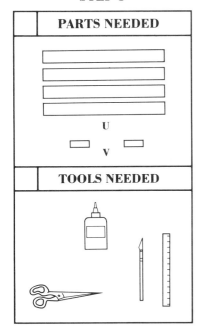

STEP 8

PARTS NEEDED

U

V

TOOLS NEEDED

STEP 8: BUILDING THE RAILS

Cut out the four parts U and the two parts V. DO NOW.

Refer to the track view inset on exploded view 3.

Score and bend two of the parts U. Connect the two parts U end-to-end using one part V as a coupler between the two parts U. Glue part V halfway inside the end of one part U. Glue part U back-to-back using white glue. DO NOW.

Now glue the exposed half of part V inside the end of another part U. Glue part U back-to-back using white glue. DO NOW.

You now have one side of the rails. Repeat the above instructions to build the other rail. DO NOW.

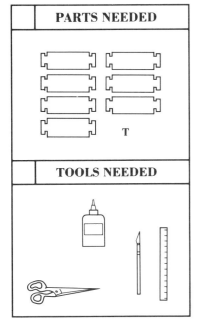

STEP 9

PARTS NEEDED

T

TOOLS NEEDED

STEP 9: BUILDING THE TIES

Cut out the seven parts T. Score and bend. Glue each part T with white glue at the tabs and let dry. DO NOW.

Use your hobby knife to score the rail mounts on top of each part T. DO NOW.

STEP 10: INSTALLING THE RAILS ONTO THE TIES

Using the spacing gauge, attach the ties to the rails (parts U). Use white glue to attach the rail mounts on the ties to the rails. Attach a tie to each end of the rails before installing the middle ties. DO NOW.

CONGRATULATIONS!

You can now place your locomotive and tender box onto the rails and ties for display.

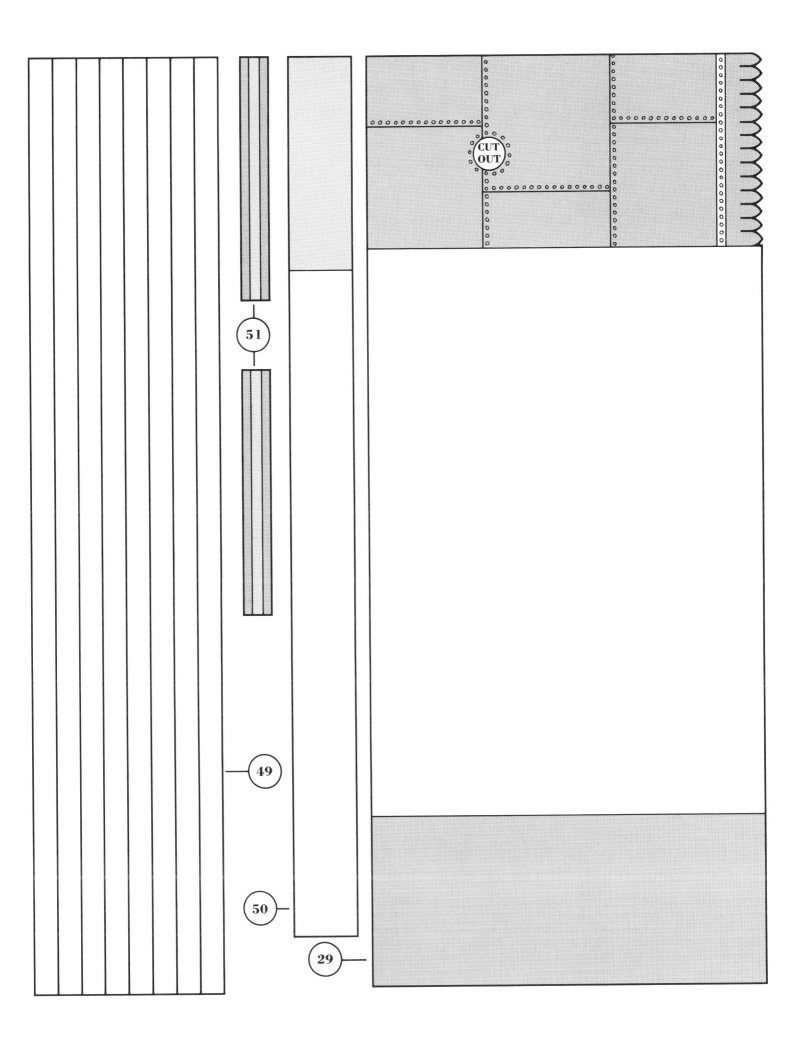

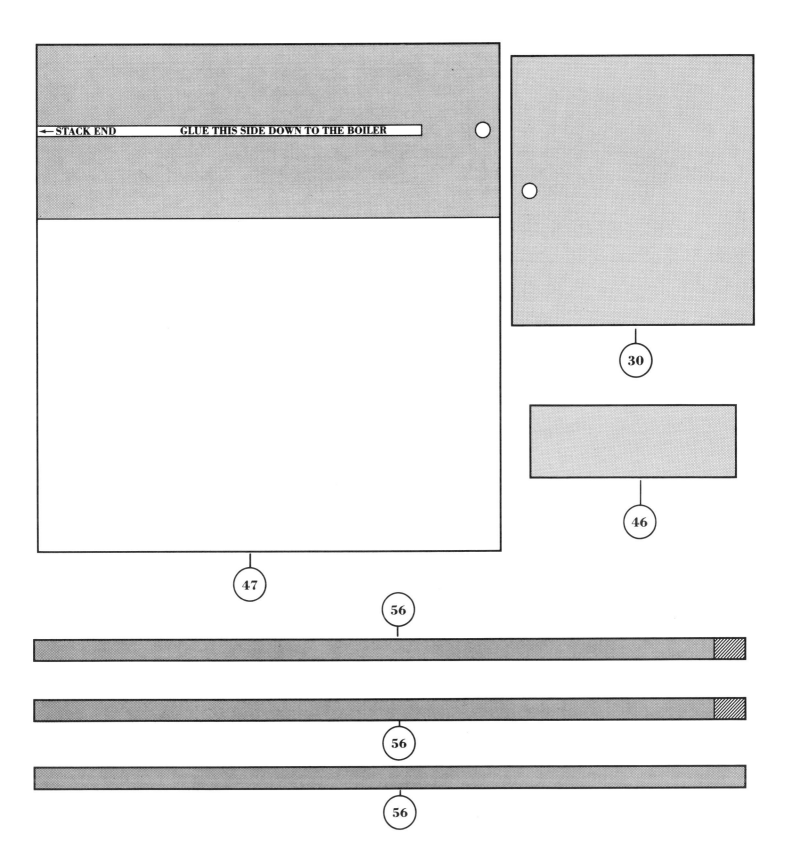

← STACK END   GLUE THIS SIDE DOWN TO THE BOILER

30

46

47

56

56

56

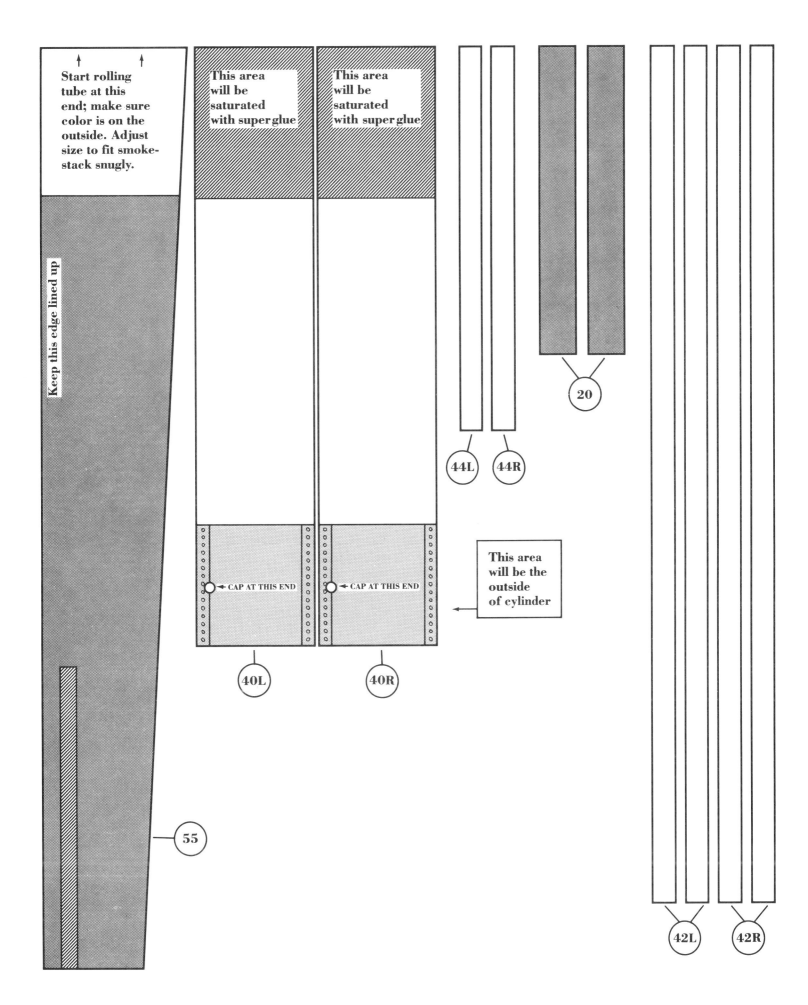

Start rolling
tube at this
end; make sure
color is on the
outside. Adjust
size to fit smoke-
stack snugly.

Keep this edge lined up

This area
will be
saturated
with super glue

This area
will be
saturated
with super glue

◄— CAP AT THIS END

◄— CAP AT THIS END

This area
will be the
outside
of cylinder

20

44L

44R

40L

40R

42L

42R

55

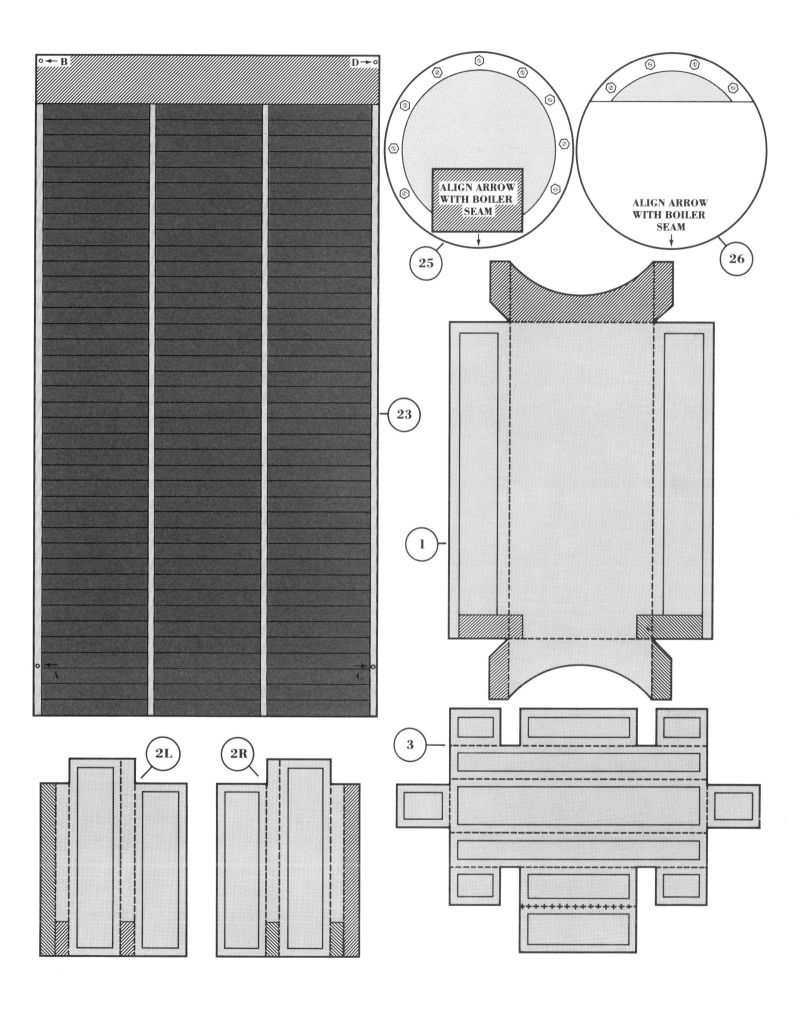